CRISIS IN UKRAINE

VOLODYMYR ZELENSKYY

Jill C. Wheeler

Abdo & Daughters
MIDDLE GRADE NONFICTION
An imprint of Abdo Publishing
abdobooks.com

ABDOBOOKS.COM

Published by Abdo Publishing, a division of ABDO, PO Box 398166, Minneapolis, Minnesota 55439. Copyright © 2023 by Abdo Consulting Group, Inc. International copyrights reserved in all countries. No part of this book may be reproduced in any form without written permission from the publisher. Abdo & Daughters™ is a trademark and logo of Abdo Publishing.

Printed in the United States of America, North Mankato, Minnesota.

052022

092022

THIS BOOK CONTAINS RECYCLED MATERIALS

Editor: Tamara L. Britton

Series Designer: Laura Graphenteen

Cover Photographs: Anadolu Agency/Contributor/Getty Images; Shutterstock Images

Interior Photographs: ALEXEY DRUZHININ/Contributor/Getty Images, p. 7; American Photo Archive/Alamy Stock Photo, p. 46; Anadolu Agency/Contributor/Getty Images, pp. 44-45, 47, 56-57; Antonio Masiello / Contributor/Getty Images, p. 6; Associated Press/AP Images, pp. 13, 53; Handout/Handout/Getty Images, pp. 59, 61; Insidefoto srl/Alamy Stock Photo, pp. 50-51; NurPhoto/Contributor/Getty Images, pp. 32-33; Future Publishing/Contributor/Getty Images, pp. 42, 43; Omar Marques/Stringer/Getty Images, p. 54; Pacific Press/Contributor/Getty Images, pp. 14-15; Russian Government/Alamy Stock Photo, pp. 34, 35; SERGEI GAPON/Contributor/Getty Images, p. 28; SERGEI SUPINSKY/Contributor/Getty Images, pp. 23, 24-25; Shutterstock Images, pp. 45, 9, 10-11, 22, 26-27, 29, 37, 38-39, 49; SOPA Images/Contributor/Getty Images, p. 8; VLADYSLAV MUSIENKO/Contributor/Getty Images, pp. 20-21; Wikimedia Commons, pp. 16-17, 18, 30, 40; WOJTEK RADWANSKI/Contributor/Getty Images, p. 55

Design Elements: Shutterstock Images

LIBRARY OF CONGRESS CONTROL NUMBER: 2022934966

PUBLISHER'S CATALOGING-IN-PUBLICATION DATA

Names: Wheeler, Jill C., author.

Title: Volodymyr Zelenskyy / by Jill C. Wheeler

Description: Minneapolis, Minnesota : ABDO Publishing, 2023 | Series: Crisis in Ukraine | Includes online resources and index.

Identifiers: ISBN 9781532199141 (lib. bdg.) | ISBN 9781098273125 (ebook)

Subjects: LCSH: Zelenskyy, Volodymyr, 1978- --Biography--Juvenile literature. | Presidents--Biography--Juvenile literature. | Ukraine--Politics and government--Juvenile literature.

Classification: DDC 947.710--dc23

TABLE OF CONTENTS

A Ukrainian soldier walks along a row of armored personnel carriers as the military prepares to defend itself against a Russian invasion.

CHAPTER ONE

ROLE OF A LIFETIME

The evening of Wednesday, February 23, 2022, was tense in Ukraine, a country in eastern Europe. Ukrainian journalists reported a sense of tension and disbelief among the people. Around the world, many wondered whether this would be the day neighboring Russia would invade Ukraine. It would be a long night for Ukrainian president Volodymyr Zelenskyy.

Since November, satellite photos had recorded images of Russian soldiers gathering on the Ukrainian-Russian border. Now, over 100,000 Russian troops and their weapons sat waiting there. That night, the Russian government had released a statement. It said pro-Russian separatists in eastern Ukraine requested military assistance from Russia.

Ukraine's president
Volodymyr Zelenskyy

Several hours later, Zelenskyy gave a live address. He spoke to both the people of Ukraine and the people of Russia. Zelenskyy said he had just called Russian president Vladimir Putin. The result, Zelenskyy said, was silence. Zelenskyy then began an appeal to the Russian people to seek peace, not war. "I speak to you not as a president, but as a citizen of Ukraine," Zelenskyy said. "Your leadership has approved their step forward into the territory of another country. This step—this step could be the beginning of a big war on the European continent."

The live address was a gutsy move by the Ukrainian president. Zelenskyy's story was different from the one Russian citizens heard from their leaders. Zelenskyy pointed out the shared border and shared experiences of people in Russia and Ukraine. He called attention to their shared culture. He talked about how common it was for families to have loved ones in both countries. He stressed that Ukraine did not want war. Then he warned that if Ukraine was attacked, its citizens would fight back.

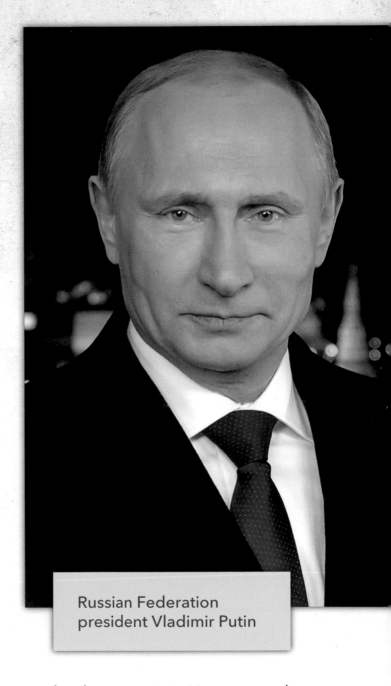

Russian Federation president Vladimir Putin

Shortly after five o'clock in the morning on February 24, the Russian invasion began. It would become the largest conflict to take place in Europe since World War II. It would also be the latest high-profile stage for the comedian and actor turned Ukrainian president, Volodymyr Zelenskyy.

Before he was elected president of Ukraine, Zelenskyy had never held public office. He rose to fame as a comedian, a performer, and an actor who made fun of politics and politicians. He turned a funny television series about government corruption into a political career working to fight it. After his election, he was dragged into the global spotlight during a major US political scandal.

With the crisis in Ukraine, Zelenskyy emerged as the face, heart, and voice of Ukrainian resistance. He appeared in videos from

Zelenskyy performs at a comedy show just days before being elected Ukraine's president.

After the Ukrainian Army liberated the city from Russian occupation, Zelenskyy went to Bucha to survey the damage.

the front lines of the battle for the capital, Kyiv. In the videos, he rallied his nation, taunted his enemies, and encouraged his allies. Zelenskyy is a master storyteller and communicator who often has surprised his critics. His journey from comedy to wartime president is a story of hope, change, and challenge.

The city of Kryvyi Rih is located were the Saksahan and Inhulets rivers meet. When Ukraine was part of the USSR, it was home of Kryvorizhstal, the nation's largest metal production facility.

CHAPTER TWO

"VOVA"

Volodymyr Oleksandrovych Zelenskyy was born on January 25, 1978, in Kryvyi Rih, Ukraine. Then, Ukraine was the Ukrainian Soviet Socialist Republic. It was part of the Union of Soviet Socialist Republics (USSR). Zelenskyy's father, Oleksandr, was a computer science professor and a natural comic. His mother, Rymma, was trained as an engineer. They lived in a neighborhood called Kvartal 95.

Like most Ukrainians then, Zelenskyy spoke Russian. But unlike most Ukrainians, Zelenskyy and his family were Jewish. Kryvyi Rih was in a region to which many Jewish people were exiled during czarist Russia. More than 5,000 Jews were killed there during the Holocaust, including three of Zelenskyy's great-uncles. Zelenskyy's family and friends called him "Vova."

When Zelenskyy was 13 years old, the USSR collapsed. Ukraine became an independent nation. By then, Zelenskyy's hometown was in decline. Kryvyi Rih had earlier been a center for iron mining and steel production. But by the early 1990s, its citizens struggled with unemployment, alcoholism, and crime.

UNION OF SOVIET SOCIALIST REPUBLICS (USSR)

In 1917, there was a revolution in the Russian Empire. After a civil war, the Union of Soviet Socialist Republics was formed on December 29, 1922. The USSR was the first country based on the communist system of government. The Ukrainian Soviet Socialist Republic was a member of the union from the USSR's outset until its collapse in 1991.

As a teen, Zelenskyy enjoyed English rock music. He played for tips on the streets of Kryvyi Rih, but a gang member smashed his guitar. Zelenskyy told his friends what had happened. He joked that Ukraine was not yet ready for him.

Such humor became a salvation for Zelenskyy and his friends. They became fans of a television show called *K.V.N.* In English, the name meant "Club of Funny and Inventive People." The show started in Russia in the 1960s and quickly became popular. It featured contests to be the funniest person.

Soviet-era public art in Kryvyi Rih depicts steelworkers in honor of the city's industrial past.

Zelenskyy's high school, School No. 95, planned a *K.V.N.*-style competition in 1994. It would be students versus teachers. Zelenskyy was the captain of the students' team. He boldly predicted that the student team would win. And the students indeed pulled it off.

Zelenskyy performs a routine during a concert at Studio Kvartal 95.

CHAPTER THREE

KVARTAL 95

Zelenskyy and his friends' comedy triumph seized upon a big change in Ukraine. As part of the USSR, Ukrainians could not publicly criticize the government. Now, Ukraine was independent. People were free to make fun of problems in government. Zelenskyy and his friends would use this new freedom to explore Ukraine's emerging comedy and performing arts scene.

In 1995, Zelenskyy enrolled at the local campus of Kyiv National Economic University. He wanted to study the performing arts. His mother was concerned a performing arts career would make it difficult for him to make money. Zelenskyy wanted to address his mother's concerns, so he enrolled in the law program. Two years later, he formed Studio Kvartal 95, a comedy contest team. With the team, Zelenskyy began what would become a pattern of poking fun at the political elite in the name of laughs.

During this time, Zelenskyy began dating another talented comedy writer, Olena Volodymyrivna Kiyashko. Kiyashko also had grown up in Kryvyi Rih. She and Zelenskyy did not know each other well until university. Kiyashko eventually changed the focus of her studies from architecture to writing. She became a full partner in Studio Kvartal 95.

Some members of Studio Kvartal 95 went on to serve in Zelenskyy's presidential administration.

Kyiv National Economic University ranks number three among Ukraine's universities.

That same year, Zelenskyy landed a spot on *K.V.N.* He became a regular performer there, even as he continued studying law. Zelenskyy graduated in 2000, but he did not begin a law practice. He had already found success producing scripts and screenplays for local companies.

In 2002, Studio Kvartal 95's live sketch comedy caught the attention of Ukraine's largest television network. The Kvartal 95 performers soon found themselves with a prime-time slot. Their *Evening Quarter* program was similar to the US sketch comedy show *Saturday Night Live.*

Evening Quarter took aim at everyone. Sketches made fun of Ukrainian political heroes and villains alike. They poked fun at wealthy oligarchs and humble traffic police. The show's audience grew to include political figures on both sides of key issues.

Meanwhile, Zelenskyy and Kiyashko decided to become more than just professional colleagues. They married on September 6, 2003. They also founded the Studio Kvartal 95 production company that year. It would become a successful business.

Zelenskyy expanded from sketch comedy to film in 2005. He wrote and starred in a musical-comedy version of *The Three Musketeers.* He later cowrote and starred in a string of popular romantic movies in Ukraine. One of those featured the young star as a New York City dentist. In 2006, Zelenskyy showed off his athletic talents too. He won the Ukrainian version of *Dancing With the Stars.*

Igor Kolomoisky owned a large share of 1+1 Media Group. The company owned the 1+1 channel that aired *Servant of the People*.

CHAPTER FOUR

SERVANT OF THE PEOPLE

Zelenskyy briefly left Studio Kvartal 95 in 2011 to become general producer of the Ukrainian television network Inter TV Station. Upon returning to Studio Kvartal 95, he made a joint production agreement with Ukrainian television network 1+1. That deal introduced him to Igor Kolomoisky. Kolomoisky was one of the wealthiest people in Ukraine. He was also a member of the oligarchy. Kolomoisky would become one of Zelenskyy's biggest supporters as he made a career in politics.

By this time, Zelenskyy had become a minor celebrity. He often played well-meaning but bumbling leading men. He wrote and starred in television shows and movies. He was also the voice of Paddington Bear in the Ukrainian versions of *Paddington* and *Paddington 2*.

As Zelenskyy's career advanced, he and his fellow Ukrainians were living in a changing society. Ukraine continued to struggle with its past as part of the communist USSR, even as it moved toward democracy. Zelenskyy began to work on his fluency in the Ukrainian

Paddington is a British film that was nominated for two British Academy Film Awards.

Ukrainians often protest government corruption. Here, protestors oppose allowing people involved in corruption investigations to run in parliamentary elections.

language. He, like many others, also began to question the way things were done in Ukraine. He was especially interested in the influence of the oligarchy on Ukraine's government.

A turning point in Zelenskyy's career came in 2015. It was the start of the television series *Servant of the People*. In the series, Zelenskyy played a high school history teacher named Vasiliy Holoborodko. Holoborodko goes on a rant about government corruption. Unknown to Holoborodko, his passionate speech is recorded on a mobile phone and goes viral. This sets off a series of events that leads the teacher to be elected to public office.

Servant of the People ran for three seasons on the 1+1 network. In 2016, Netflix picked up the hit show for distribution outside of Ukraine. Servant of the People became popular due to the way it addressed the problem of corruption in Ukraine's government. Government officials made decisions that benefited themselves or their friends instead of ordinary citizens. As viewers watched Zelenskyy's character work to root out corruption, they began to think. Many started to wonder what life could be like for them without government corruption. Zelenskyy was thinking about that, too.

Zelenskyy shooting an episode of Servant of the People. The series ran for three seasons before Zelenskyy was elected president of Ukraine.

Petro Poroshenko was elected Ukraine's president in 2014. He had previously served as Minister of Foreign Affairs and Minister of Trade and Development.

CHAPTER FIVE

FICTION MEETS REALITY

In 2018, Zelenskyy decided to act on his growing desire to end government corruption. Studio Kvartal 95 officially registered Servant of the People as a political party in Ukraine. On December 31, 2018, Zelenskyy officially entered the presidential race. He was one of 39 candidates. Ukrainians elect a president every five years by popular vote.

Before December 31, most observers believed the presidential race would be a contest between current Ukrainian president Petro Poroshenko and former prime minister Yulia Tymoshenko. Zelenskyy's candidacy changed that.

Poroshenko had been successful in building up the military. He also had been successful at gaining international support for Ukraine's

Zelenskyy and his wife Olena celebrate the election result.

struggles against Russia. Despite these gains, Ukrainian citizens were frustrated by slow economic growth, poverty, and corruption.

Zelenskyy's campaign was unlike any other in Ukraine's history. He did not make any in-person campaign appearances. He did not talk to journalists. He did not give speeches. He did not travel around the country meeting with voters. Instead, he addressed voters through videos on YouTube, Instagram, and television.

Zelenskyy continued acting in comedy routines and in *Servant of the People*. These activities allowed him to avoid detailed descriptions of what he would do if he were president. He focused instead on very general dissatisfactions felt by many Ukrainians. He talked about needing to stand up to Russia. He talked about corruption and how it hurt the economy.

Zelenskyy's campaign strategy worked. He won the election in a landslide on April 21, 2019. He became not only the youngest president in the history of Ukraine but also the only Jewish head of state at that time outside of Israel. The election meant *Servant of the People* had made history, too. It became the only known fictional show to end because it became true.

Zelenskyy defeated Poroshenko *(left)* with more than 70 percent of the vote.

President Trump and President Zelenskyy at the 74th UN General Assembly in New York City on September 25, 2019. They took questions from reporters about their call, which Zelenskyy said was "good."

Zelenskyy's inauguration speech acknowledged his beginnings in comedy. It also promised future commitment. "Throughout my entire life, I've tried to do everything so Ukrainians smiled," he said. "In the next five years, I will do everything so that you, Ukrainians, don't cry."

As president, Zelenskyy inherited an ongoing five-year war with Russia in eastern Ukraine. That conflict had claimed more than 10,000 lives. He also inherited a government structured on the corrupt influence of wealthy oligarchs. Zelenskyy's television character had railed against such corruption. Now, Zelenskyy had to find ways to make real change.

That challenge was quickly tested. On July 25, 2019, Zelenskyy was on a telephone call with US president Donald Trump. At first, the two compared notes about their similar situations. Both had worked in television before winning public office. During the call, President Trump asked Zelenskyy to look into whether former vice president Joe Biden worked to remove a prosecutor who was investigating a Ukrainian gas company with ties to Biden's son Hunter.

Months later, the content of the call became public. Some believed Trump sought the information to smear Biden in Trump's upcoming reelection campaign. The call led to impeachment proceedings against President Trump. The US House of Representatives voted to impeach Trump. However, he was found not guilty in a trial in the US Senate and remained in office.

Zelenskyy had not expected that his conversation with Trump would become public. Yet the phone call highlighted the difficult position of the new Ukrainian president. Ukraine had for years relied on US support to fend off ongoing pressure from Russia. Zelenskyy feared he would lose that support if he refused President Trump's request.

In January 2020, US secretary of state Mike Pompeo *(left)* traveled to Ukraine to meet with President Zelenskyy. Pompeo assured him that President Trump's impeachment had not soured relations between the countries.

CHAPTER SIX

MOUNTING CRITICISM

As the scandal unfolded in the US, Zelenskyy told reporters he did not want to get involved in American politics. Privately, he and his administration were becoming more and more worried. The US Congress had approved nearly $400 million in aid to Ukraine. Yet the money had not been delivered. Testimony in Trump's impeachment trial indicated he had frozen the aid to Ukraine in July 2019. The testimony also suggested that President Trump planned to keep the aid from Ukraine if his request was not honored.

Meanwhile, Zelenskyy found himself in a virtual stalemate with Russia. Talks to resolve the ongoing conflict between the Ukrainian government and Russian-backed separatists over the Donetsk and Luhansk oblasts in the

Donbas region were going nowhere. In September 2019, Ukraine and Russia exchanged prisoners after a long series of negotiations. The talks then stalled over disagreements about how elections should be run in the Donbas. Some experts suggested the Russians hoped to take advantage of Zelenskyy's political inexperience to get what they wanted.

The fall of 2019 also saw Zelenskyy under fire for his relationship

In December 2019, *(left to right)* President Zelenskyy, German chancellor Angela Merkel, French president Emmanuel Macron, and Russian president Vladimir Putin met to discuss the conflict in the Donbas. No agreement was reached.

with Ukrainian oligarch Igor Kolomoisky. Many believed Kolomoisky had paid for Zelenskyy's presidential campaign. The US Federal Bureau of Investigation (FBI) began checking into whether Kolomoisky had committed financial crimes. These included allegedly cheating a Ukrainian bank out of billions of dollars. Zelenskyy cut his ties to the oligarch to demonstrate his commitment to ending corruption.

Zelenskyy achieved some early successes shortly after his election. He and his administration took steps to make about 500 state-owned companies instead be privately owned. He worked to remove a ban on selling farmland. This would allow individual farmers to purchase land owned by the government. He also took steps to make it difficult for wealthy oligarchs to make money from unfair loans.

As his presidential term continued, it became clear that reform would not happen quickly. Lawsuits against corruption were blocked in the courts. Zelenskyy appointed many government officials who were inexperienced, just like he was. He hoped this would lead to less corruption. The political novices were in fact more honest. But their inexperience also led to mistakes.

This became clear in the Ukrainian health-care system. Zelenskyy's administration wanted to improve health care. Then the COVID-19 pandemic hit. Few Ukrainians chose to get vaccinated. In November 2020, Zelenskyy became ill with COVID-19. He publicly received his vaccination in 2021. However, by the end of 2021, Ukraine had the lowest COVID-19 vaccination rate in all of Europe. The government was unable to convince a majority of Ukrainians to get the vaccine.

Ukraine's farmland is valuable. The country is a leading grain producer, exporting 95 million tons (86 million metric tonnes) in 2021. It is known as the Breadbasket of Europe.

Zelenskyy denied that he used offshore companies to avoid taxes. A spokesman said the companies were set up to protect against corruption in previous governments.

CHAPTER SEVEN

SINKING APPROVAL

On October 3, 2021, Zelenskyy found himself in another scandal. The Pandora Papers is a collection of documents that reveal the hidden owners of expensive assets. These assets include secret bank accounts, works of art, and companies set up in foreign countries to avoid taxes. The International Consortium of Investigative Journalists leaked the documents.

Zelenskyy's business holdings had been discussed during his campaign. Most people knew he owned a media and entertainment business. However, the documents revealed Zelenskyy and partners in his comedy production business owned multiple companies based in other countries.

Zelenskyy and his partners used those companies' funds to invest in expensive real estate in London, England. They then funneled the profits from those investments back through the foreign companies. This avoided having to pay taxes on the profits in Ukraine.

The Pandora Papers ignited a public debate about whether Zelenskyy was really the different kind of president he said he was.

By fall 2021, only 35 percent of Ukrainians approved of the job he was doing.

By September of that year, Zelenskyy had reached out to two different US presidents to seek support against Russian aggression. So, many were surprised when he began to downplay threats of a Russian invasion at the end of that year. In early February 2022, Zelenskyy asked Western governments to tone down their talk of war. He brushed off reports from United States spy agencies that suggested Russia was getting ready to invade. He

THE PANDORA PAPERS

The International Consortium of Investigative Journalists is an independent network of journalists. It is based in Washington, DC, but has offices around the world. The group released the Pandora Papers beginning October 3, 2021. The papers exposed secret offshore accounts including those of 35 current and former world leaders. The papers showed the 29,000 accounts may hide an estimated $32 trillion from taxation.

Many foreign embassies closed, but France's ambassador to Ukraine, Etienne de Poncins *(left)*, remained in Ukraine. He moved the French embassy from Kyiv to Lviv on February 28. It reopened in Kyiv on April 17.

told journalists to stop talking about a potential invasion. He said doing so threatened the Ukrainian economy.

Zelenskyy also criticized staff members of foreign embassies who were leaving Ukraine as tensions mounted. "Diplomats are like captains," Zelenskyy said. "They should be the last to leave a sinking ship. And Ukraine is not the *Titanic*."

Planes at Boryspil International Airport near Kyiv were regularly disinfected to stop the spread of COVID-19.

Zelenskyy's critics were quick to point to his lack of political experience as the prewar crises mounted. Ukraine was battling a record wave of COVID-19 infections as well as the threat of a Russian invasion. In response, Zelenskyy launched a campaign to provide smartphones to Ukrainian senior citizens who were vaccinated.

The events merely added to criticisms of Zelenskyy and his administration. He had been criticized for not standing up to Russia. His pledge to address corruption and reform the judicial system seemed to be getting nowhere. His business dealings were not unlike those of the oligarchs he claimed to oppose. Perhaps most frightening for many Ukrainians, he showed no obvious preparation for a Russian invasion. It seemed no one knew what they would do if an invasion took place.

By October 2021, Zelenskyy's approval rating among Ukrainians had fallen to less than 25 percent. The rating reflected the belief on the part of many Ukrainians that Zelenskyy had not kept his promises. All of that changed on February 24, 2022.

On February 23, 2022, Zelenskyy met with Poland's president Andrzej Duda (left) and Lithuania's president Gitanas Nauseda (right). They signed a declaration that Ukraine should be a candidate to join the EU.

President Zelenskyy gave a speech in Kyiv on February 28 to update the Ukrainian people on Russia's invasion of their country.

CHAPTER EIGHT

"I AM HERE"

The Russian invasion of Ukraine began early in the morning on Friday, February 24. Russian bombs lit up the sky before dawn around the capital city of Kyiv. As Ukrainian citizens sought shelter, their president took to the airwaves once again. Just hours before, Zelenskyy had appeared in his signature blue suit and tie. This time he appeared in an olive drab T-shirt. Dark circles under his eyes indicated he had not slept. "Now is an important moment," he said. "The fate of our country is being decided."

As fighting continued into Saturday, Zelenskyy posted on social media. He asked Ukrainians not to believe messaging coming from Russia. He filmed a video of himself to show he remained in Kyiv. "I am here," he said. "We are not putting down arms." Stating that truth was their weapon, Zelenskyy vowed that the Ukrainian people would continue to fight for freedom.

The same day, the Ukrainian embassy in Britain posted on its Twitter account that the US offered to get Zelenskyy out of Ukraine. But he refused. "The fight is here," Zelenskyy reportedly told US embassy officials. "I need ammunition, not a ride."

Zelenskyy also released a short video acknowledging that his life and the lives of his family members were in danger. "I am staying in government quarters together with others," he said. "The enemy has designated me as target number one, and my family as target number two." Zelenskyy's and his wife Olena's daughter, Oleksandra, was born in 2004. Their son, Kyrylo, was born in 2013. All of them remained in Ukraine in a secret location.

Zelenskyy met with European leaders to develop a plan of action against Russia's invasion.

While separated by the invasion, Zelenskyy and his wife could communicate only by phone.

As the days wore on, Zelenskyy continued to use Twitter, Facebook, and Instagram to dispute Russian messages. He told stories and posted videos of what was happening in Ukraine. He posted notes of support from around the world to let Ukrainians know they were not alone. He urged people everywhere to take action against Russia.

The number of followers of the official Ukrainian social media channels surged. Millions of people around the world began watching the crisis in Ukraine. By the middle of March, the official Ukrainian Twitter account had a record 1.9 million followers. Zelenskyy's Instagram followers had increased by more than 6.5 million. Perhaps most importantly, Zelenskyy's message and requests for help were heard far beyond the Ukrainian border.

Within weeks of the conflict's start, governments around the world had punished Russia with more sanctions than any other country in history had received. Russian banks were removed from the SWIFT system. This meant they were unable to do business with the rest of the world. The US also sanctioned the company that was building a natural gas pipeline to connect Russia and Germany. Major

SWIFT

The Society for Worldwide Interbank Financial Telecommunication (SWIFT) is a secure messaging network through which international payments are sent. It allows countries to make safe business transactions with one another. When Russia's banks were disconnected from SWIFT, they became unable to send or receive secure international payments.

McDonald's closed all of its 850 locations in Russia. The company also closed all 108 stores in Ukraine for safety reasons.

businesses, including McDonald's, Starbucks, and Coca-Cola, announced they were stopping their work in Russia. Apple, IKEA, and Nike said they would no longer sell their products there.

In a March 22 virtual meeting with the Italian Parliament, Zelenskyy asked lawmakers to seize Russian leaders' real estate, bank accounts, and other assets.

CHAPTER NINE

FROM THE BUNKER

In early March, there were rumors of threats against Zelenskyy's life. One report said Zelenskyy had survived three assassination attempts in a matter of days. The report said anti-war groups within Russia's Federal Security Service had helped Zelenskyy's own security officers learn the assassination plans. Despite surviving the attempts, Zelenskyy moved his video briefings away from Kyiv's landmarks. He began to film from locations that were harder to identify.

The death threats did little to hinder Zelenskyy's appeals to other world leaders for help. He continued to post videos and host news conferences from secret locations. On a video conferencing platform, he spoke with the US Congress, the Canadian Parliament,

NO-FLY ZONE

The military operation no-flight zone (NFZ) is known to the general public as a no-fly zone. An NFZ establishes an area in which enemy aircraft cannot fly. If aircraft appear in the zone, they will be shot down. Russian president Vladimir Putin warned against such a move, saying it "will be considered by [Russia] as participation of the respective country in an armed conflict."

the British Parliament, the European Parliament, and the Japanese Parliament, among others. He spoke passionately of the need for unity to stop the Russian attack. At times, he brought audience members and even his translators to the brink of tears. On March 4, he told thousands of Europeans, "If we win, and I'm sure we'll win, this will be the victory for the whole democratic world."

In his March 16 address to the US Congress, Zelenskyy recalled the attack on Pearl Harbor in 1941. He also spoke of the 9/11 attack as a time when innocent Americans, like Ukrainians in early 2022, were killed. He asked for a no-fly zone over Ukraine to prevent Russian bombing attacks. He urged more sanctions against Russia. He also asked for technology to help fight Russian missile attacks. He thanked the US for its support while also asking it to do more. This was the first time anyone addressed Congress from a war zone.

Zelenskyy's March 4 address was broadcast in cities across Europe. Here, several thousand people gather at the Römerberg in Frankfurt, Germany, to watch.

Almost six million refugees had left Ukraine by May 1, 2022. Here, some of the three million who fled to Poland live in a temporary shelter.

In each address, Zelenskyy carefully considered his message. He used historical events and leaders from particular nations in his speeches. He used humor where possible. He shared video footage from the war zone to show the conflict's reality. He also appealed to the values and ideals of each nation he addressed. He used his addresses to highlight the similarities between those values and the values of the Ukrainian people.

A Ukrainian couple embrace in relief after crossing the border at Medyka, Poland.

At the Screen Actors Guild Awards in late February, several celebrities also cited shared values with Zelenskyy. Actors Michael Keaton and Brian Cox both urged unity with Zelenskyy as a colleague. "I will tell you, we have a fellow actor in Zelenskyy, who deserves some credit tonight for fighting the fight," Keaton said while accepting an award.

President Zelenskyy visits troops in the Donetsk oblast in the Donbas.

CHAPTER TEN

MAN FOR THE MOMENT

Zelenskyy's wartime leadership has been compared to that of Winston Churchill. Churchill was the British prime minister during World War II. He famously rallied his people during the darkest days of the war. A skilled writer, Churchill created a persona for the moment. He inspired his nation to fight on. His presence on rooftops during air raids in a black bowler hat became a symbol that all would be okay.

Zelenskyy's social media posts and videos played a similar role for a world on the brink of the unknown. On March 24, Zelenskyy took to Twitter with a video marking one month since the invasion began. In his nightly address, he asked viewers to stand up—wherever they were—for Ukraine and for freedom. "The world must stop the war," he said. "Come to your squares, your streets. Make yourselves visible and heard."

As a wartime president, Zelenskyy was challenged on multiple fronts. He had to reach out to allies for support and assistance. He stressed the importance of preventing further war. He had to remain open to talks with Russia to reduce the war's duration and death toll.

Zelenskyy also had to make difficult decisions. He had declared martial law on February 24, 2022. Martial law is used during times of emergency. It temporarily transfers power from civilian authorities to military officials.

On March 20, Zelenskyy banned the activities of 11 political parties that opposed Ukraine's government. He banned all private television stations as well, turning instead to a single, state-run channel. These moves were intended to reduce opportunities for people in Ukraine to support the Russian war effort. They also made Ukraine look much like the authoritarian enemy it was defending against.

In 2019, during the third season of *Servant of the People*, the show's fictional Ukraine has split into multiple territories. While the show is fiction, the various territories could easily represent the separatist territories in eastern Ukraine. They could represent those who would pit Ukrainian speakers against Russian speakers. They could stand for the tension in Ukraine between its Soviet past and a desired future of democracy.

Regardless of the cause, Zelenskyy's *Servant of the People* character delivered a speech that fit the moment both then and years later. "Enough with the old slogans that cleave our land apart," he said in the show. "East, west, north, south, we're one country, we're all Ukrainians."

On May 1, 2022, speaker of the US House of Representatives, Nancy Pelosi, met with President Zelenskyy in Kyiv to confirm the United States' commitment to helping Ukraine.

TIMELINE OF VOLODYMYR ZELENSKYY

"I was honored to spend a few minutes talking with President Zelenskyy—the Winston Churchill of our time—this morning. I thanked the president for his leadership, his example, and his commitment to liberty, and I saluted the courage of the Ukrainian people."

—Former US president George W. Bush

JANUARY 25, 1978
Volodymyr Zelenskyy is born in Kryvyi Rih, in the Ukrainian Soviet Socialist Republic.

1995
Zelenskyy enrolls in Kyiv National Economic University.

1978

1991

1991
The USSR collapses; Ukraine becomes an independent country.

1995

1997

1997
Zelenskyy forms the Studio Kvartal 95 comedy team; he lands a spot on the *K.V.N.* program.

DECEMBER 31, 2018
Zelenskyy officially enters the presidential race.

JULY 25, 2019
Zelenskyy speaks with US President Trump; the call leads to Trump's impeachment.

FEBRUARY 24, 2022
Russia invades Ukraine; Zelenskyy declares martial law.

2018

2019

2022

2019

2021

APRIL 21, 2019
Zelenskyy is elected president of Ukraine.

OCTOBER 3, 2021
The Pandora Papers are released; Zelenskyy's approval rating drops.

US defense secretary Lloyd Austin *(left)* and US secretary of state Anthony Blinken *(right)* visit President Zelenskyy to show support for Ukraine.

2000
Zelenskyy graduates from university.

2015
Servant of the People premieres.

SEPTEMBER 6, 2003
Zelenskyy and Olena Kiyashko marry; they found the Studio Kvartal 95 production company.

2018
Studio Kvartal 95 registers Servant of the People as a political party.

MARCH 4, 2022
Zelenskyy's virtual address is broadcast to cities across the EU.

MARCH 20, 2022
Zelenskyy bans opposition political parties.

MARCH 16, 2022
Zelenskyy addresses the US Congress.

MAY 1, 2022
Speaker Nancy Pelosi meets with Zelenskyy in Kyiv.

GLOSSARY

assassinate – to murder a very important person, usually for political reasons.

asset – something of value owned by a person, a business, or a government.

bunker – a shelter dug into the ground to keep people safe from attack.

communism – a social and economic system in which everything is owned by the government and given to the people as needed. A person who believes in communism is called a communist.

corruption – dishonesty or improper behavior.

culture – the customs, arts, and tools of a nation or a people at a certain time. Something related to culture is cultural.

czarist – the government of Russia under the czars. Czars ruled Russia until the 1917 revolution.

democracy – a governmental system in which the people vote on how to run their country.

designate – to indicate and set apart for a specific purpose, office, or duty.

elite – of or relating to the best of a class.

embassy – the residence and offices of an ambassador in a foreign country.

exile – the state or a period of forced absence from one's country or home.

fluent – able to speak clearly and easily in a certain language.

Holocaust – the killing of millions of Jewish people and others by Nazi Germany during World War II.

impeach – to charge a public official for crime or misconduct in office.

inaugurate – to swear into a political office.

martial law – military rule imposed on the general population during a war or other emergency.

oblast – a political and administrative division within a country.

oligarch – one of the rulers in an oligarchy, or group of wealthy people using their money for governmental influence.

persona – the personality that a person such as an actor or politician projects in public.

prime time – the time of day when television audiences are the largest, historically between 8:00 and 11:00 p.m.

propaganda – media made and distributed to aggressively promote or damage a cause or group.

sanctions – an action by several nations against another nation to force it to obey an international law.

satellite – a manufactured object that orbits Earth. It relays scientific information back to Earth.

separatist – an advocate of separatism, a belief in, movement for, or state of separation such as schism, secession, or segregation.

stalemate – a state of inaction resulting from the opposition of equally powerful persons or factions.

ONLINE RESOURCES

Booklinks
NONFICTION NETWORK
FREE! ONLINE NONFICTION RESOURCES

To learn more about Volodymyr Zelenskyy, please visit **abdobooklinks.com** or scan this QR code. These links are routinely monitored and updated to provide the most current information available.

INDEX